Rookie
Read-About® Geography

Great Salt Lake

By Mary Schulte

Subject Consultant
Robert E. Ford
Professor of International Sustainable Development and Social Policy
Loma Linda University, Loma Linda, California

Reading Consultant
Cecilia Minden-Cupp, PhD
Former Director of the Language and Literacy Program
Harvard Graduate School of Education
Cambridge, Massachusetts

Children's Press®
A Division of Scholastic Inc.
New York   Toronto   London   Auckland   Sydney
Mexico City   New Delhi   Hong Kong
Danbury, Connecticut

Designer: Herman Adler Design
Photo Researcher: Caroline Anderson
The photo on the cover shows salt-covered boulders in the Great Salt Lake.

Library of Congress Cataloging-in-Publication Data

Schulte, Mary, 1958–
  Great Salt Lake / by Mary Schulte.
      p. cm. — (Rookie Read-About Geography)
  Includes index.
  ISBN 0-516-25034-5 (lib. bdg.)   0-516-29703-1 (pbk.)
  1. Great Salt Lake (Utah)—Juvenile literature. 2. Great Salt Lake (Utah)—
Geography—Juvenile literature. I. Title. II. Series.
  F832.G7S34 2006
  979.2'42—dc22   2005021247

JE
SCH
C.1

7/06

CHILDREN'S PRESS, and ROOKIE READ-ABOUT®,
and associated logos are trademarks and/or registered trademarks
of Scholastic Library Publishing. SCHOLASTIC and associated logos
are trademarks and/or registered trademarks of Scholastic Inc.

1 2 3 4 5 6 7 8 9 10 R 15 14 13 12 11 10 09 08 07 06

Can you float on water?

You can easily float on the Great Salt Lake in Utah.

The lake is saltier than any ocean. The salt makes the water dense, or heavy.

You can float on the Great Salt Lake because you are less dense than the water.

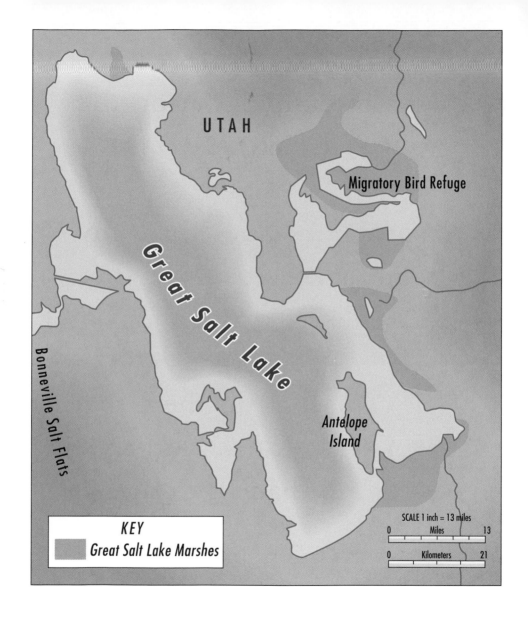

UTAH

Migratory Bird Refuge

Great Salt Lake

Bonneville Salt Flats

Antelope Island

KEY
Great Salt Lake Marshes

SCALE 1 inch = 13 miles

0   Miles   13

0   Kilometers   21

5

The Great Salt Lake was once huge, prehistoric Lake Bonneville. Over time, much of the water in Lake Bonneville dried up.

The Great Salt Lake and the Bonneville Salt Flats remain. High-speed cars now race at the flats.

Explorer Jim Bridger was probably the first white person to see the Great Salt Lake. Local Native Americans had likely already seen it.

Bridger spotted the lake in 1824. He believed he had reached the Pacific Ocean.

9

The Great Salt Lake is North America's largest saltwater lake. It is about 75 miles (121 kilometers) long and about 30 miles (48 km) wide.

The lake is shallow. In most places, it is only about 20 feet (6 meters) deep.

The Great Salt Lake is a terminal lake. This means that no water flows out of it. This is part of the reason the lake is so salty.

13

Rain clouds over the Great Salt Lake

Rivers and streams flow into the lake. They carry salt. Rain and snow add water, too.

Some of the water evaporates. Heat causes it to change from a liquid to a gas. It's as if the water disappears! But the salt from the water remains behind.

Companies harvest salt from the lake. They collect lake water in big, shallow ponds.

The heat from sunshine makes the water evaporate. Workers collect the salt that is left behind.

Salt being harvested from the Great Salt Lake

Salt from the lake is not pure enough to eat. But it has other uses. It is used to make salt for icy roads.

It is also pressed into salt-lick blocks. Animals lick these blocks to take in nutrients. The nutrients help the animals stay healthy.

The Great Salt Lake is so salty that no fish live in it. Brine shrimp are the only animals that can survive there. Brine shrimp are about the size of your fingernail.

Workers gather brine shrimp eggs. The eggs are then used as fish food.

Brine flies buzz along the Great Salt Lake. Millions of birds eat the brine shrimp and brine flies.

Birds nest in the Great Salt
Lake's marshes.

The lake has a refuge where people can bird-watch. A refuge is an area where wildlife is protected.

The Great Salt Lake's bird refuge

The Great Salt Lake has eleven islands. Antelope Island is the largest.

Antelope Island

About 600 buffalo live there.

Visit the Great Salt Lake!

Float on the water or ride in a kayak. Bike or hike on island trails. Or grab your binoculars and join the bird-watchers.

Words You Know

Antelope Island

Bonneville Salt Flats

brine shrimp

buffalo

Jim Bridger

terminal lake

Index

About the Author

Mary Schulte is a newspaper photo editor and author of books and articles for children. She enjoys writing for children and hopes to do the photography for her books someday. She has written one other book in the Rookie Read-About® Geography series. She lives and works in Kansas City, Missouri.

Photo Credits

Photographs © 2006: Alamy Images: 29 (Jerry & Marcy Monkman/EcoPhotography.com), 10 (Worldwide Picture Library); AP/Wide World Photos/Salt Lake Tribune: 27, 31 top right (Rick Egan), 24 (Al Hartmann); Corbis Images: 9, 31 bottom left (Bettmann), 6, 22, 30 bottom (George D. Lepp), 13, 31 bottom right (David Muench), 14 (Jim Richardson), cover (Scott T. Smith), 21, 31 top left (Douglas P. Wilson/Frank Lane Picture Agency); Getty Images/Joel Sartore/National Geographic: 25; Peter Arnold Inc./S.J. Krasemann: 18; Photri Inc./M. Gibson: 17; Superstock, Inc./David Muscroft: 3; Tom Till Photography, Inc.: 26, 30 top.

Map by Bob Italiano